THE GREEN MONTH

THE GREEN MONTH

MATTHEW FRANCIS

The Green Month

faber

First published in 2025
by Faber & Faber Ltd
The Bindery, 51 Hatton Garden
London EC1N 8HN

Typeset by Hamish Ironside
Printed in Wales by Gomer Press

A CIP record for this book is available from the British Library

ISBN 978-0-571-39454-8

MIX
Paper | Supporting
responsible forestry
FSC
www.fsc.org   FSC® C114687

Printed and bound in the UK on FSC® certified paper in line with our continuing
commitment to ethical business practices, sustainability and the environment.
For further information see faber.co.uk/environmental-policy

Our authorised representative in the EU for product safety is
Easy Access System Europe, Mustamäe tee 50, 10621 Tallinn, Estonia
gpsr.requests@easproject.com

10 9 8 7 6 5 4 3 2 1

Acknowledgements

My principal source for these versions has been the literal translations and notes produced by the University of Wales's Dafydd ap Gwilym Project, available on the website https://dafyddapgwilym.net. Extracts from Dafydd ap Gwilym's poetry used in the Introduction are taken from *The Poems of Dafydd ap Gwilym* translated by Joseph P. Clancy (Bath: Brown Dog Books, 2016) and *Nine Thorny Thickets: Selected Poems by Dafydd ap Gwilym* translated by Rolfe Humphries (Kent, OH: Kent State University Press, 1969). I am grateful to Dr Simon Rodway and Professor Dafydd Johnston for giving me the benefit of their expertise on Dafydd and medieval Welsh poetry in general, to Lavinia Greenlaw for her detailed feedback, and, as always, to Creina Francis for being my first reader. The liberties I have taken with the texts and any errors I may have introduced are, however, my own responsibility.

Acknowledgement is due to the following publications in which some of the poems first appeared: *Dream Latin* (Broken Sleep Books), *New Welsh Review*, *Poetry Wales*, the *London Magazine*, the *Poetry Review*.

Contents

Introduction

Dafydd ap Gwilym's poem 'Merched Llanbadarn' ('The Girls of Llanbadarn') describes a typical medieval scene: the poet is attending mass at his parish church, not far from the modern town of Aberystwyth. It is full because Christianity is ubiquitous and church-going compulsory. Everyone is wearing their best clothes. But if we expect a glimpse into the spirituality of a more pious age, we are in for a surprise. Dafydd has turned his back on the altar to get a better look at the girls in their finery. My version of the poem is 'Church' on p. 14 of this book. Like the others here, it's a reworking of the original rather than a faithful rendering, so I'll quote instead from Joseph P. Clancy's translation:

> No Sunday in Llanbadarn
> I'd not be, and others condemn,
> With my face towards a graceful maiden
> And my nape towards gracious God.

Sexuality is a central theme of Dafydd's work, and one of the reasons many modern readers find him easy to relate to. He is part of a long tradition of explorers of male heterosexual desire, which includes Donne, Rochester, Berryman and his own literary hero, Ovid. In some ways it's a more difficult subject than the respectable one of love: to deal with it honestly is not just to celebrate its fulfilment but to confess weaknesses and transgressions, failures and the loss of dignity. No poet has done this more unflinchingly or with more wit and charm than Dafydd ap Gwilym. In 'The Girls of Llanbadarn', for example, the objects of his voyeurism have no trouble putting him in his place. Not only do we see the girls from Dafydd's point of view, but we also see him from theirs: a pale, long-haired dandy. They are not impressed, and indeed he tells us with tongue-in-cheek irritation that he has never had his way with any of them.

The theme of comic sexual failure runs throughout his work. In 'Trafferth Mewn Tafarn' ('Inn', p. 13) he arranges an assignation with a girl he meets on his travels, only to cause chaos by bumping into the furniture in the dark and getting himself mistaken for a thief. 'Y Cwt Gwyddau' ('Geese', p. 15) begins with a romantic encounter and ends with the poet cornered by an angry goose. These events, actual or invented, fit the conventions of the time, in this case the genre of the *fabliau*, or humorous tale of ordinary life. There is, however, an element of self-examination, of what a later generation would character- ise as 'confessional' writing, that sets Dafydd apart. It's present in the unflattering self-description in Llanbadarn Church, and there's an even more extreme example in 'Y Drych' ('Mirror', p. 37), describing his appearance as prematurely aged by love and suffering. Other poems take this introspection still further: a sigh becomes a meditation on breath, and he finds himself listening to his own heartbeat. Most strikingly and controver- sially, in a poem rejected by shocked scholars for centuries but now accepted as canonical, he apostrophises his own penis ('Y Gal' / 'Prick', p. 40).

If I've concentrated so far on the comic and earthy aspects of Dafydd's work, it's only to make the point that he writes about the totality of sexual experience. Like other medieval authors, including his younger contemporary Chaucer, he is not mealy- mouthed, and for this reason he sometimes speaks to us more directly than love poets of later periods. At the same time, though, his very determination to tell us everything can emphasise the differences between then and now. One of the most unexpected is that, for him, sex was a largely outdoor activity.

Much of his best work relates to his affair with a married woman, Morfudd, the wife of a man he calls *Y Bwa Bach*, or 'the Little Bow', possibly because he was a hunchback.

Adulterous love was a conventional theme of the verse of his time, but the details Dafydd gives about this relationship are enough to convince most readers that it really happened and was central to his life. In fact, we learn more from him about what it was actually like to commit adultery in the Middle Ages than from any other source I can think of. There was little privacy in the medieval home, where everyone slept together for warmth, so if you wanted to make love in secret, it was necessary to go outside. This meant that it was only usually possible to conduct an affair in spring and summer, when the weather was warm enough. (Suddenly it becomes clear why so many of the poets of the past celebrated spring as the season of love.) In the Welsh countryside, which was much more heavily wooded than it is today, trees offered both shelter and privacy. Again and again, he depicts himself waiting for Morfudd in the setting he describes as *Y Deildy*, or 'the house of leaves' ('Glade' p. 4).

This combination of passion and the natural world gives Dafydd's poetry its distinctive atmosphere. The ecstasies, frustrations and mishaps to which any illicit relationship is subject typically take place against a background of foliage with birds and animals as audience and supporting cast. This is another element that makes him seem modern: waiting in his glade for Morfudd to turn up, he has plenty of time to observe his surroundings, which he describes with a warmth and attentiveness we hardly expect to see in a poem before the nineteenth century. Holly and hawthorn, wind and wave, a stag, a lark, a crow and a trout are addressed, among many others. Again, there is an element of the conventional here; in medieval Welsh poetry it was usual to enlist a bird or animal as a 'love messenger' to communicate with his beloved, and Dafydd's deer, lark and trout are used in this way while in one of his finest poems the wind itself carries the message ('Y Gwynt' / 'Wind', p. 20). Similarly, the crow ('Y Frân' / 'Crow', p. 19) is valued as a love-helper, acting as an early-warning system against an intrusive husband, while the wave ('Y Don ar Afon Dyfi' / 'Wave', p. 32) is a love-obstacle, stopping him from reaching Morfudd. But conventions only feel artificial when there's no feeling behind them; when they're fully inhabited, as here, they create a poetic world. And in 'Y Draenllwyn' / 'Hawthorn' (p. 31), his affection for the mutilated tree is independent of any romantic agenda – a good case could be made for calling it one of the first ecopoems.

Dafydd ap Gwilym is both a supreme artist of his own age and one with an enormous amount to offer to ours. It's hard to think of another poet who is simultaneously so frank, funny and passionate about sex, so lyrical and observant about nature, and so ambitious yet playful in his craft. For several reasons he is not as widely read in the English-speaking world as he should be. Not only did he write in a language that has been marginalised for centuries and actively repressed for most of that time, but he is also cut off from us by the cultural intricacies of a society very different from our own and by the technical complexity of Welsh verse. When we picture him in his professional context we must think not of books (printing, of course, had not been invented), but of a bard performing in front of a live audience to his own harp accompaniment. He was a highly skilled formal poet, whose work brilliantly met the literary expectations of the day, which were quite different from those we bring to a poem now.

I am not qualified to discuss the verse forms of *cywydd* and *englyn*, and the prosodic constraint of *cynghanedd*, the alliterative patterns unique to Welsh poetry; Mererid Hopwood's book *Singing in Chains* offers an excellent introduction to the subject. I have, however, written poetry in many different forms and have a good sense of what technical constraints do to meaning. A poem's form is not intended to cancel itself out, leaving as little impression on the text as possible. On the contrary, it actively contributes to meaning, forcing the poem away from its author's original intention. The dialectic of form and content is a demonstration of the poet's prowess, a struggle we are meant to appreciate and applaud. In an age dominated by free verse, it's easy to overlook this. A constraint such as rhyme can lead inexperienced poets into a dead end; they need to learn to dance with it rather than follow wherever it takes them. This doesn't mean that the constraint itself is bad, or that they shouldn't allow it to exert an influence.

Dafydd wouldn't have composed the poems he did if he hadn't been working in set forms. Ignoring this aspect of his work has two undesirable consequences: one obvious, the other much less so. The obvious thing is that we miss out on his ingenuity, the showmanship which is such an important part of his personality. The less obvious is that we are left with a lot of extraneous matter originally generated by the technicalities of composition but which, in their absence, seems awkward and inexplicable. Typical of these indigestible lumps are the parenthetical phrases called *sangiadau*. In the introduction to *The Poems of Dafydd ap Gwilym*, Clancy cites an example from 'The Girls of Llanbadarn':

> From too much looking, stern lesson,
> In back of me, sign of weakness,
> It happened to me, friend of powerful song,
> To bend my head without a single companion.

'In the first three lines,' Clancy points out, 'the forward movement of the sentence is concentrated in the first half of the line, with the second half providing a kind of running parenthetical commentary.' We might describe this odd syntactic structure as a rhetorical convention, but Clancy cites Sir Thomas Parry, the great authority on Dafydd, to the effect that it originates in the technical demands of Welsh metre. I've occasionally noticed something similar when modern poets attempt to write a sestina (that demanding troubadour form in which the end words of the first stanza recur in a different order as end words of each subsequent stanza); sooner or later, most practitioners find themselves having to accommodate an end word they don't want, and resort to throwing in a superfluous line which repeats or summarises something said earlier.

Clancy retains the *sangiadau* in his translations. There is no other option if a translator is determined to be faithful to what Dafydd wrote. But I would argue that literal translations of this kind, even when refined by precise diction and stylistic elegance, are not really faithful at all. They present the poet as a historical oddity, someone we have to make allowances for, imagining what his poems would be like if we were the sort of people for whom he originally wrote, speaking his language and sharing his culture. They are not so much poems as placeholders indicating what the poems were for other readers in other times. When I first read Dafydd in the translations of Clancy, Rachel Bromwich and others, the strangeness of his thought processes and their expression left me intrigued and frustrated in equal measure. That changed for me one day when I came across the following passage:

Across North Wales
The snowflakes wander,
A swarm of white bees.
Over the woods
A cold veil lies.
A load of chalk
Bows down the trees.

This is the opening of 'The Winter' by the American poet Rolfe Humphries from his collection of Dafydd translations *Nine Thorny Thickets*, and it's immediately apparent that it is not a placeholder for a poem but a poem in its own right. The short lines sing, given punch by the concluding rhyme, while the string of metaphors for snow, so characteristic of medieval Welsh verse, would seem equally at home in a post-Imagist context. 'The Winter' appears to be one of the many poems falsely attributed to Dafydd by later copyists, but this is not true of the title poem, based on 'Y Sêr' ('Nightwalk', p. 25).

The use of rhythm and occasional rhyme in these versions reminds us that we are reading poetry, while the economical writing works well for the modern reader. Humphries has achieved this economy by taking some liberties with the original. 'Nine Thorny Thickets' is about half the length of 'Y Sêr'. Where the original poem begins with a conventional address to the beloved, Humphries distils the background into a couple of lines, then plunges the reader into the night journey. It's an opening suitable for the impatience of the modern world, which would rather have the author start apparently in mid-narrative than waste time on preliminaries. Dafydd, on the other hand, was both an oral performer and a musical one, and live audiences need a certain amount of background information to ensure they don't lose the thread.

Humphries is not translating Dafydd in the usual sense of the word. He's rewriting him, and the best of his versions bring the work to life for me in a way that more faithful renditions fail to do. Poets have always rewritten their predecessors, and sometimes describe the result as 'after' Ovid, Ronsard or whomever. Without ever producing an actual translation, I've written poems *after* both poets (Keats, Bashō and the anonymous author of the Old English *Lacnunga*) and prose writers (Robert Hooke, Sei Shōnagon and the medieval travel writer who called himself Sir John Mandeville). Most relevant to the present project is my 2017 book *The Mabinogi*, which turned the medieval Welsh prose epic into verse, making many cuts, introducing new material, and changing both plot details and the order of the narrative. I was the latest of a long line of writers, from Evangeline Walton to Alan Garner to Gwyneth Lewis, who have used *The Mabinogi* as the source of new work, just as Shakespeare used Plutarch and Saxo Grammaticus as material for plays of his own, and those plays in turn became sources for Verdi, Bernstein and Baz Luhrmann.

Not long after publishing *The Mabinogi*, I decided to try my hand at a new treatment of Dafydd. He is, after all, my local poet: born at Brogynin, a few miles from where I live, and buried, probably, under an oak in the graveyard of Strata Florida abbey, to which I made a pilgrimage soon after coming to live in Ceredigion twenty years ago. Llanbadarn Church, where he ogled the girls, is a short walk from my house. Inspired by Humphries's reworkings and in keeping with my established approach, I chose to write poems 'after' Dafydd rather than translations – not changing the setting or period but aiming to bridge the imaginative gap between his world and that of the modern English-speaking reader. I wanted them to reflect his own formal technique, though I knew I couldn't hope to match its complexity and craftsmanship. *Cynghanedd*, notoriously, can't be made to work in English. Even the combination of short lines with rhyme that characterises his verse is very challenging, often producing a jingling, nursery-rhyme effect that can trivialise the subject matter. Humphries gets round this by using rhyme only occasionally, as ornament rather than constraint, giving the impression of a stricter form than the one he has actually adopted. For me, the obvious solution was a variation on the tapering syllabic stanza I used in *The Mabinogi*, in which each line is shorter than the one before. It's not nearly as demanding as traditional Welsh prosody but the effect is to squeeze the verse, forcing me to be more economical as I go on, while still giving me room to manoeuvre in the early part of the stanza where it may be necessary to fill in background details. I also decided to make each poem the same length, arguably a more severe constraint than the stanza itself. Each is a snapshot of one of Dafydd's themes, concentrating on the most striking images and ideas.

To compensate for the loss of the more discursive and leisurely aspects of his work, the poems combine to form a sequence, a modular dramatic monologue in which Dafydd tells us of his love affairs, misadventures, insomnia and panic attacks; gives vent to boastfulness, despair and self-criticism; celebrates the joy of 'the green month' (generally agreed to be May); and laments the bleakness of 'the black month' (November). I've compressed his various lovers into one, a sort of lyric 'she' in the manner of the lyric 'I'. While this deprives us of most of the biographical detail associated with Morfudd and his other principal lover Dyddgu, it does draw attention to the idealising aspect of Dafydd's writing about women. He is a man in the grip of an obsession, and if he were not obsessed with these particular women he would be equally so with others. He knows this as well as we do, and is more than capable of laughing at himself for it. Where love is concerned, he is capable of everything – apart from temperance.

MATTHEW FRANCIS, RHYDYFELIN CEREDIGION, 2025

THE GREEN MONTH

Calendar

The green month rides into the forest on his high horse
in a surcoat of young oak leaves, on his shield
a gold sun, splendent, and three thrushes.
But there is no one to fight –
the black days have fled

and the tents of the green month are pitched under the trees,
his palisades brambles and briar roses,
and we'll bunk down on a bed of ferns
till the evening campfire smoke
of spring mist rises.

And later when the black month rides in on his high horse
in his surcoat of rotten oak leaves, his shield
streaked with rain, sable, bearing three wolves,
he'll find the forest ruined
and the green days fled.

Glade

The wood's made ready for her. Its green bunting flutters.
She will come down that slope, the sun in my eyes,
and I'll lead her to the leaf litter
laid out for her in the room
that grows every spring.

Its beams are birch and ashwood, its walls wattled willow.
With the curtains of foliage drawn round us,
we'll be all the furniture we need.
Now the wood's clothed, all we'll wear
is the sun's motley.

A thrush in the oak gallery tunes its instrument
to welcome her back from her winter bedroom,
the clutch of her rickety husband.
No fire is lit in the hearth:
the heat comes from me.

Feathers

I asked her to weave me a garland out of snippets
pruned from the regalia of the birch trees,
a leafy coronet of forest.
Every poet should have one,
a nest for the muse.

But she wouldn't touch a leaf before the black month came
to take them all. We'd be naked without them.
She gave me this instead, a circlet
glinting with peacock feathers.
My head's a jewel-box.

I am a bird of paradise swishing my turquoise
and lapis lazuli plumage in the gloom.
I'm rich in glow-worms and butterflies,
gazed at and gazer at once,
with eyes in my hair.

Yesterday

Yesterday, she was tall and pale among the birches.
I wore her softness round me like a mantle.
Will I see any more yesterdays?
Lustrous day, no relation
to the day before.

Most days are the day before. I weather them somehow,
an old cat shivering in my scraggy fur,
the twigs of my bruised ribs sticking out.
I'm tough as the whippy shoots
of an apple tree.

Where else would you find yesterday but in a forest?
It's hard to catch, part animal, part daydream,
a white deer slipping among the trees
that comes when you've given up
to stand in the sun.

Shadow

The birch leaves in the rain seemed full of her light footsteps.
They wouldn't turn up now. She was not the shrug
of a blackbird's wing as it took off
or the dry fingertip tap
of acorn on leaf.

All that arrived late was the sun, squeezing through the trunks,
and that flat personage stretching above me,
a faceless ogre with trees for stilts,
a heron stiff in the reeds,
a black-gowned friar.

Because we're conjoined at the foot, you call yourself me,
shadow. You don't do anything without my say-so.
Bad conscience, copycat, hangover,
when I go home I am not
taking you with me.

Hay

Her door has that wooden look. Even if it opened
she wouldn't want to fish me out of the rain.
I must be seven-eighths water now
as the rest of the world is
this sodden evening.

A heap of raked-up hay in the field. I crawl inside
this hovel of thatch, a space that isn't one.
The stuff enfolds me, a blanket, cloak
and soft-haired lover steamy
with vegetable musk.

Here are as many stalks as you could wish to chew on
to ponder a poem on our flimsiness:
how flesh is grass and the scythe gets us.
Still, there are worse hereafters
than this downy place.

Window

The window's empty now. Sometimes her face appears there
striped with the wooden bars of the glassless frame
then slips away into the dark house
like the full moon into cloud
taking light with her.

I've tried to kiss her through the bars. She flinches away
and leaves me locked in the prison of outside.
What is she getting up to in there
while I can't free my eyes from
that box of nothing?

I am a strange astronomer, in love with the moon,
sleepless between the fennel and the roses,
watching a miniature square of sky
for her ivory presence
to loom into view.

Owl

The owl's noisy tonight. He won't let me say my prayers
but hoots his canticles outside my window.
This hook-footed, feathery gargoyle
scrambles my message to God
with his *oohs* and *whos*.

No point in trying to sleep. He'll be at it all night,
a creature from a folk tale, shrunken angel
bearing news from the land of the dead.
No wonder the daylight birds
don't want to know him.

I was about to go off to be alone with her
behind sleep's curtains when this insomniac
with the round eyes and revolving head
stuck his beak into my dream
and ripped it to shreds.

Insomnia

Black sleep, I need you. A light is keeping me awake.
The honeyed candle that's burning in my brain
is scorching my eyes from the inside:
the saffron flame of her hair,
her beeswax softness.

Crouched in his featherbed, the owl has nothing to say.
The whole of Wales has crept under the covers:
no bog or moorland to wander through,
only the fabric of sleep
I should be wrapped in.

The Little Bow, her crook-backed husband, growls beside her,
a hot-breathed dragon coiled around his treasure.
Is she staring at nothing, like me,
seeing her leaf-shadowed bard
in his peacock crown?

Clock

There's just room for two of us in my head, this round space
enclosed in bone and darkness, lit from within
by the afterglow of today's thoughts.
Here we can meet every night,
wherever she is.

Lissom as only a dream can be, her form flickers
in rhythm with my breath. She speaks dream Latin,
a tongue her husband can't understand,
and silently, for no sound
can penetrate here –

except the clang of a clock. Newfangled minute-mill,
nocturnal dawn chorus, sleepmason's chisel,
blacksmith's hammer bashing at blackness,
it cleaves the night into hours
where no time should be.

Inn

I lay in the house of snores. She was on the far side
of the midnight room littered with mattresses.
The burly furniture lay in wait.
I had no map of the dark
to guide me to her.

A stool bludgeoned my shin. I sent it clattering down,
but the table's legs were too many for me
and we collapsed, entwined together,
as pans catastrophed round.
I groped in a bed

and found more bodies than expected: three Englishmen
who rose, shouting, 'Thief! Welsh thief, after our packs!'
Then it was blind-man's-buff hue and cry
while I bandaged my bruised self
in the swaddling dark.

Church

I've turned my back on God. The priests will take care of him.
They're at the altar now, murmuring to him
as they fumble with the bread and wine.
Like the owl in my poem
I'm gazing backwards

at the girls of the parish, pewfuls of cherubim
who slide their glance away, rustling their plumage.
If I could only get one of them
out of this echoing stone
into soft forest!

They've seen me sideways. They're whispering to each other:
'Is that waterfall hair his or his sister's?'
'His skin is the colour of sour milk.'
I'll have to pray on my own
in my green chapel.

Geese

We had the hall to ourselves as I sat fingering
the trinkets of firelight trembling on her skin.
I told her I ached from my journey
and other things. When she smiled
the night went berserk

with footsteps and shouting, the steel shriek of a drawn sword.
I knew the sounds of an encroaching husband
and fled, searching the crannies of shadow
for the outline of a door.
Here it was at last.

I squeezed into a cupboard of feathery scuffles.
The place was spitting with geese that grabbed at me
with the toothless pliers of their beaks
like so much angry bedding.
Husbands are gentler.

Moon

I have nothing in my pockets again. That last coin
is out of reach, deep in its black velvet purse.
I watch it spending itself among
jostling stars, a clipped florin
lavished on the clouds.

Give me a darkness with body, not this tinny light
that would turn anyone into a phantom,
this sun in a mask, leaching colour
and goggling at me with that
po-faced expression.

There will be no goings-on tonight on the stark land
beneath her walls. The husband at his window
needs no nightwatchman with that lantern
laying open the bushes
where lovers might lie.

Echo

This rock is shaped like a wardrobe. A ghost lives in it
weaving the stream to liquid polyphony
and breeding mad cats out of the wind.
A few drops of rain drum up
a gravel hailstorm

and every word you utter is an incantation.
Call out to a girl and the heavens hear it
a hundredfold, and when she arrives
you might be having a tryst
with the seraphim.

We lay in the crook of the stone, the lap of the stream.
Whatever I whispered the ghost got hold of
and rattled her with resounding words
until she fled, leaving me
to talk to myself.

Dawn

We made a nest in the night of bodies and bedding.
Who knew where the dark ended and we began?
We were two and one and manifold
behind the window's closed eye
till light opened it,

a vague intrusion in the room in its grey nightgown.
It might have been the moon, but she said morning.
I said that crow's ratchet cry was caused
by the fleas in its feathers
not the itch of dawn.

Then all the dogs of the countryside savaged the air.
I told her they bark in their sleep but she said,
'Make for the woods before they catch you.
Come back tonight when it's safe
to delve in the dark.'

Crow

Bird made of shadow, you fly across the sun
as your other self is darkening the grass,
and people shiver at your passing.
We frighten you in return
with a man of sticks.

But I bless the grindstone of your voice, high in your tree,
when I'm curled at the root in a nest with her
and the dawn wakes you, or her husband
thrashing the bush with his men.
Either way, I'm off.

Stout bundle of bird with your shining horn of a beak,
heaven preserve your legs from snares and birdlime
as they stump in the leaf-sludge. Feel free
to probe in our furrowed fields
for green worms of wheat.

Wind

Who sent you, messenger, running without any feet
all puff and scurry but never out of breath?
First you're all over me, then you're off
over the next hill before
I've laid eyes on you.

Don't waste your sighs on me. There's a song in you somewhere
among all those leaves and seeds, the pocket-fluff
you carry in the folds of yourself.
Sing it around her house where
my voice can't reach her.

Trespasser traipsing through cornfields, no one can stop you.
Berserker havocking among oak branches,
you play in the surf, whippersnapper,
a restless host to the rain
that nests in your hair.

Gull

Pillowy bird, plumped up on the sea's crumpled covers,
you rise and fall in your sleep, as if the waves
rolling beneath were breathing through you.
However whitely they break,
you stay, clump of foam.

Climb up on the wind, a snippet of wave against blue,
pageboy slipping between lordly skirts of clouds
but always leaning towards elsewhere
uttering the *why-why-why*
of a stranded soul.

From up where you are, she is only a swerve away.
Can you see the curve of the coast, the castle
presiding over the rising tide?
Slide to her, cry your question,
bring me her answer.

Trout

Slippery being, most cantankerous of suppers,
one flexing limbless muscle, breaker of nets,
you loom to me now at the lake's edge
and utter your silent word,
the poet's vowel, O.

Bird without wings, you should be flying in some river,
half-air, half-water, a helter-skelter home.
Swallow your way upstream, leapfrogging
knucklebone rocks, through the forks
of this veiny land.

You'll find her on the riverbank, dissolving her gaze
in water as if longing to be elsewhere.
She'll read my words in your speechlessness,
the shining globules that rise
and burst in the air.

Stag

You with the crown of horns, twitching your white rump at me,
grey cleric in the cloister of the forest,
rock-tiptoer, king-of-the-castle,
you with the saplings of legs,
prince among nibblers,

knight with the crooked lances on your head, you wrestle
brain-to-brain, branch-bashing storm among birches,
for your seigneurial nuzzling-rights
over a court of soft-cheeked,
wide-nostrilled damsels.

So run to mine, almost a thought yourself, in and out
of the blink of oak trees, the trunks of sunlight,
graze at her edgewood, and startle her
like something she's forgotten
that's still there, waiting.

Lark

Never really at home in your bothy of grasses,
you climb a ladder of song to the attic.
Now you've become geometrical,
an abstract point from which lines
of sound radiate.

You're safe perched on the topmost branch of a tree of cloud.
No jealous husband's arrows can hit you there –
they would lose heart and fall back to earth –
so you can sing her my words
and she will listen.

I've used more conspicuous envoys, dowdy angel,
but none that can embroider the atmosphere
like you, with your filament of voice.
Sing her a tune that she can't
shake out of her head.

Nightwalk

I crossed the road to the moor. She was on the other side
of the ninefold darkness I must struggle through,
my feet hooked by briars, guzzled by bog.
I'd lost a country round here,
kept stubbing my toes

on its granite bulges. Black humps of hill forts loomed round,
stray flibbertigibbets flared in the marshes –
not the lights I was after. But then
I reached a crest. Overhead
were acres of stars.

Look at them! Shiny as cherries, hanging in clusters,
they are the brass nail heads in the oak of night,
a coffer of farthings, gilded saints,
candles the wind fans brighter
and cannot blow out.

Star

I need no messenger to go before me through the dark town.
No one will see me as I pass their windows
without lantern or torch to her house.
That's just the way I am now,
crazy till daybreak.

The candle that God made lights me, October-gale-proof,
unquenchable by any midnight cloudburst,
Heaven's little pearl on its high shelf
where no thief can get at it.
I need that one star.

Prickle of dew, crumb of white bread on an oak table,
clear-eyed late riser, it waits outside for me
as long as it takes, then we sneak home
under the cover of dawn
to sleep through the day.

Fog

Yesterday was Thursday. I walked over the high moor,
a glut of Thursday fields spread out below me
and in the distance the darker fuzz
of Thursday afternoon's woods
where I would meet her.

It all went soft as I looked. The woods whitened like hair
and wisps of fur capered around my ankles
until I tripped over nothing much.
The path was blocked by a fog
that breathed in my face.

I was smothered in fleece, a tick in the weather's wool,
cobwebbed and hung in a neglected corner,
only this unwritten-on receipt,
a scroll of parchment to show
where Thursday had been.

Journey

At Maidengrove the path was hot coals under my feet
but somehow I reached the birdless fields of Swan.
No one heard my shout at Blethin's Wood
and I forded the Saleg
thigh-deep in cold rage.

I passed through Dafydd's Gap, and crossed Crookback. At Rimstone
the valley opened its overlapping greens
and I pressed on, hunched like a gosling
poking among the cornstalks,
to get to Hoodbridge.

I skulked, a grey monk, before the gates of Ifor's Court.
My feet knew Coalbrook's slopes without me. At last
there in our leaf lair at Alderclump,
shadowy in her black cloak,
she asked where I'd been.

Bog

It's dark as bog-water tonight. The will-o'-the-wisp
of her before my eyes is my only torch –
no use to my horse. Under his hooves
a more substantial darkness
gulps and ungulps us.

We're close to the Underworld here. It's sucking at us
with its many mouths as we lurch between them,
its chill breath smelling of tar, a kiss
I'd rather slither out of
and take the long way.

Then the earth dissolves in a splash of hooves and snorting.
Some fish pond in hell. Cold rises to my knees.
If we ever flounder out of this
I'll wash my kersey stockings
and stay home at night.

Bramble

It was dark in the woods. I had to make my own path
from whatever I found there: bracken, leaf-sludge,
all grist to the wanderer's treadmill.
She was the sunlit clearing
I struggled towards.

This must be how flies feel, wrapped up in thickety web.
At least no wolves could get at me – just a root
that snatched at my ankle and threw me
down a mud slope to a hell
of vegetable fire.

Who would have thought the undergrowth had so many teeth?
No blackberry is worth fighting that bush for.
You've signed your name in blood on my skin,
snaggle-toothed spawn of a snake
and a fishing line!

Hawthorn

All year you stand on your slope in the same straight-backed pose,
your dozens of fingers spread, your hackles raised.
Only your outfit changes: green lace
and scented cream silk in spring,
autumn's coral beads.

You can look after yourself with your hidden weapons,
you with more treasure than an Englishman's shop,
so who's taken an axe to your roots,
stiff soldier of the edgelands,
and lopped half your limbs?

Whoever it is has a poet to reckon with!
I have thorns, too. Tell him to watch out for rhymes.
The coward has made me so angry
that I've written a poem
with no girl in it!

Wave

I've reached the river at last but the sea's playing there
and she's on the far shore of what used to be
a dozen feet of sluggish water.
Wave with the sun in your curls,
I must cross over.

Who let you out of the ocean to froth and frolic
among the meadows between me and my home,
an odyssey away from me now?
I glimpse its mythical blur
through your salt spittle.

Wave, patron of fishermen, lavish with your silver,
grey-cloaked galloper over shaggy pasture,
you bow before me, sweep off your cap
but you don't know your own strength.
Get down, let me pass.

Ice

Her house is armed to the teeth. Icicles bristle
above my head as I shiver at her door.
One lackadaisical arrow drops.
She's locked in behind winter's
glassy portcullis.

The river's a white road now. As I set foot it groans
as if under a hundred trundling cartwheels.
A crack zigzags across the surface
and I am plunged through the shell
into slush-water.

Oat-husks and thistles, a crop of frost in the snowfields.
There is a clear glue hardening on my walls,
clutching my fingertip like birdlime.
From now on nothing will move
but the skidding wind.

Hare

She streaks out from the bush, a grey smudge in white breeches.
Hounds scatter wailing like a mad funeral,
scrabble-slithering on the clay bank
and dunking their hindquarters
in the woodland stream.

Wind's little sister, she jinks round the invisible
obstacles on the margin of the cornfield,
and the hounds are all over themselves
snapping at where her rump was
three dodges ago.

Her bed's a dent in the ground. Running is where she lives,
this small magician. Thin air's her element.
You can bay after her all you like
but she's already elsewhere –
beloved quarry.

Fox

Squatting in front of his hole, red ember against black,
he looked like a fire demon hell had coughed up,
panting a laugh as I drew my bow
until the yew snapped in three
and I stood unstrung.

He was a smoky fire in daylight, sun in his fur,
a shrunken dragon smouldering between myths,
a lick and flicker that would flare up
later, crossing the farmyard
in the mucky dusk.

Then watch out, hens! The gentleman in the gamey coat
has a nose for feathered flesh. Men may chase him
for fifty furlongs, but he'll be back
sniffing around your bedroom.
I know how he feels.

Ruin

Scatter-boned house on a scruff of land at the field's edge,
it barely has two stones to rub together.
The moor wind whinges from room to room
but all weather's welcome here
as I used to be.

It must have taken fairy magic to unbuild this.
I wouldn't have thought the wind was up to it.
That brawling bully had just enough
breath to snuff out the hall fire
and shoo off its smoke.

Ash stirs in the black heather roots. I sat here often,
singing my poems in the nook of shadow,
the fire's small sun scorching my right cheek
while the flame of her warmed me
from the other side.

Mirror

That can't be my face lurking in there, that yellowed page,
the scar scrawled down one cheek, nose like a razor,
those last autumnal tussocks of hair
that the comb hasn't raked out.
I was good-looking

till someone submerged me beneath this speckled surface.
You might as well study yourself through pondweed.
Who is this blotchy gawp of a mask
trapped in a disc of silver,
the man in the moon?

Someone should tell the Merlin who magicked this device
from tarnished spoons and offcuts of frozen pond
that it's stopped working, or my face has.
Love will do that to a man
as well as mirrors.

Breath

I heard somebody sigh just now. It must have been me.
I left my mouth ajar and a breath slipped out.
There is a lot more where that came from,
a pressure inside my ribs.
I'm stifling with air.

I have more of it in me than a blacksmith's bellows.
I am blocked-up bagpipes, pregnant with a gale
that could strip the leaves from a forest,
I've swallowed a thundercloud
and the storm's rising.

Once I had just enough to extinguish a candle
and mutter an epigram, a whisper's worth.
They say a girl takes your breath away.
This one is welcome to mine –
there's too much of it.

Heart

Fidgety occupant, you're making more flutterings
than a whole roost of starlings under my ribs,
when there's just one of you tapping there,
a wingless, featherless chick
unhatched from the egg.

I'm tired of carrying you. You have no head for drink
and the smile of a girl sets you off again,
a foxhound scrabbling to be let out.
They say you're made for loving –
you're addled enough!

Where would I be without you? You keep me company
when the candle's out with your whispered drumming,
and I wake to your knock at my door
though you're already inside,
most intimate guest.

Prick

You've done it again, haven't you? I thought you were safe
where I'd left you, curled in the dark of my drawers.
How did that clenched eye of yours see, through
layers of linen and wool,
a glimmer of girl?

Loose end, you're always starting something. Even asleep,
mauve-faced as a newborn, swaddled in wrinkles,
your bald chicken-neck stirs in its nest
at the mere sound of her name.
One twitch and you're up,

a conger-eel rampant, seeking the clammy places,
varicose archbishop in your purple pomp.
Soldier, you gasp out your hot insides
and the world's peopled, and I'm
in trouble again.

Sun

Shepherdess of the sky tending her cumulus flock,
gold snarl on the face of the dandelion,
droplet of light on the web of day –
I have stared at her too long
and my eyes water

till it seems she's everywhere, the sting and spark of her
floating in front of everything I look at,
far off on her cloudy battlements,
and when she slips below them,
the day sinks with her.

I cannot hold her, a pan hot from the kitchen fire.
She's burned me so many times that I treasure
the soreness after she's disappeared
off to the bed where she sleeps
behind the world's wall.

Holly

Green halberdiers bristling in the woods, armed at all points,
they have the steely shine they wore as they watched
over our leaf-litter lovemaking
though only a tattered sheet
of snow lies there now.

Layers of spiked barricades and portcullis branches
guard a stronghold that has nothing inside it
but the twilight that filled it in May
and a disturbance of birds
raiding the berries.

This winter pantry of the forest, the organ loft
for the wind's solos, the choir stall of thrushes
and vaulted hall trophied with antlers
will be looking after spring
until we come back.